HEALING
MANDALAS

26 INSPIRING DESIGNS PLUS 10 BASIC
TEMPLATES FOR COLOURING AND MEDITATION

LISA TENZIN-DOLMA

WATKINS PUBLISHING

LONDON

A PATH TO WHOLENESS

AS WE REST OUR GAZE UPON A MANDALA, THE MIND BECOMES AS STILL AS THE SURFACE OF A POOL OF WATER. FROM THE PROFOUND DEPTHS OF SUCH TRANQUILLITY EMERGE INSIGHTS THAT HELP US TO TAP INTO AND DEVELOP OUR INNATE HEALING POWERS. MANDALAS CAN ALSO MAKE US MORE WHOLE BY STRENGTHENING OUR CONNECTION WITH OUR ESSENTIAL NATURE.

Mandalas most often take the form of a circle – a shape that represents the self, the Earth, the Sun, the cosmos and the state of wholeness that is the ultimate aim of mandala meditation. By taking this path we move toward a state of completeness and a realization of our true nature, which, like the circle of the mandala, is boundless and perfect. Experiencing such a deep sense of unity can be an immensely healing experience.

Healing is synonymous with "becoming whole" – attaining a state of internal and external harmony. To heal, we must bring imbalances in the mind and spirit back into a state of equilibrium, which in turn has a positive effect on the body. However, mandala meditation is about much more than this: it also makes us feel more complete by taking us on a journey of self-realization.

The unique pressures of modern living make the need for healing more prevalent now than ever. As we work longer hours, commute further and often don't take enough time to eat healthily, exercise or unwind, so the statistics for stress-related illness rise. The high expectations that we set ourselves strain our physical, mental and emotional resources, and may lead to physical symptoms, relationship problems or a generalized sense of lack of fulfilment. All are messages we should take notice of and act upon.

Fortunately, body and mind have an immense capacity for self-regeneration. And if we slow down and withdraw within ourselves, we can create space for this. Try this experiment. Clench your fist and see what happens. You probably feel tense and trapped. Then relax your hand. Do you feel more open, more receptive? The same principle applies to the mind. When your mind is stressed and cluttered, your body will feel tense; but when your mind is quiet, your body will follow suit, relaxing in a way that allows your innate healing processes to begin their work.

Healing begins at a profound level that we cannot control consciously. It might feel spontaneous and immediate, like a cog slipping into place. Or it might evolve over time. Mandala meditation allows you to encourage healing at a pace that is right for you. By setting aside a little time every day to look at a mandala – ten minutes is ideal initially – you will take the first steps on a journey away from anxiety and stress toward the increased balance, optimism and freedom

"HEART IS THE PLACE IN WHICH ONE FINDS
A REPOSE IN PURE LIGHT
AND PURE CONSCIOUSNESS."

ABHINAVAGUPTA

(C.950—1020 AD)

"IF YOU WANT OTHERS TO BE HAPPY, PRACTISE
COMPASSION. IF YOU WANT TO BE HAPPY,
PRACTISE COMPASSION."

HIS HOLINESS THE 14TH DALAI LAMA

(BORN 1935)

"YOU MUST BE A LOTUS, UNFOLDING ITS PETALS
WHEN THE SUN RISES, UNAFFECTED BY
THE MUD WHERE IT IS BORN."

SAI BABA

(1838—1918)

"OUR LIVES ARE LIKE ISLANDS IN THE SEA, OR
LIKE TREES IN THE FOREST, WHICH CO-MINGLE
THEIR ROOTS IN THE DARKNESS UNDERGROUND."

WILLIAM JAMES

(1842—1910)

The sky and the oceans provide a suitably relaxing background for a healing mandala,
since both have positive symbolic overtones. The sky suggests freedom, ease of movement and
spirituality – the awareness, perhaps, that gives us strength to deal with imperfections in our lives.
The sea provides weightlessness – an easing of burdens – as well as suggesting the endless resources
of the unconscious mind. Creatures such as birds (cranes in this example) can function as
"power animals", serving the meditator as agents of healing or transformation.

that come from reconnecting with your inner resources and gaining a fresh perspective on life's challenges.

The mandalas in this book give you routes toward your still centre. You can use them to draw emotional and spiritual sustenance from your inner well-spring. Spending time with these mandalas brings healing from the inside out as you boost your self-esteem, learn to recognize your inner beauty and strength, enhance your creativity, confront your fears, and embrace change. Wholeness, peace and wisdom come within your reach.

When selecting a mandala in this book to colour in and use for meditation, just opt for one that appeals really strongly to you. All the mandalas are presented as line drawings. The first 26 designs, which are complex and sophisticated, are followed by a selection of basic geometrical templates you can elaborate to create your own design. Once you have chosen your mandala, let the recommended colour palette guide you in deciding how to colour it in; or alternatively, choose your own colours, following your intuition. When your mandala is coloured to your personal preference, you can begin your meditation.

Meditation relies heavily on concentration, so before using a mandala that you have coloured in, find a quiet place to sit, far from distractions or noise. Try to absorb the peaceful atmosphere around you and focus initially on stilling your mind, breathing slowly and deeply. Use the following step-by-step guide as a prompt to good practice.

HOW TO MEDITATE ON MANDALAS

1. With the chosen mandala placed on a table or on the floor at arm's length in front of you, perhaps on an improvised easel, level with your eye-line, sit comfortably – either on a chair with your feet flat on the floor, or on a cushion with your legs crossed.

2. Breathe slowly and deeply, from the diaphragm, while emptying and stilling your mind.

3. Gently gaze at the mandala and relax your eyes so that, initially, the image goes slightly out of focus.

4. Sitting quietly, concentrate on the image fully and allow its shapes, patterns and colours to work on your unconscious mind. If distracting thoughts arise, let them drift away and gently bring your focus back to the mandala.

5. Do this for at least 5 minutes initially. In later sessions, gradually try to build up your meditation period to 15 minutes.

6. When you are ready, slowly bring your attention back to the world around you.

PERFECT SYMMETRY

THIS MANDALA, CENTRED ON THE PROMISE OF A FLOWER AND ITS SEEDS, CAN HELP THE MEDITATOR TO GO BACK SYMBOLICALLY TO THE MOMENT OF CREATION, FINDING WHOLENESS IN THE ESSENCE OF BEING. WE ARE REMINDED THAT THERE IS NO FUNDAMENTAL DIFFERENCE BETWEEN SUBJECT AND OBJECT.

1   Appreciate the shapes of the mandala. Start with the banded triangles, denoting the physical world. Turn next to the concentric circles, embodying all-embracing spiritual perfection. Note the "tear splashes" around the edges, whose shape suggests joy and sorrow.

2   Look at the triangles radiating from the middle in different directions. These represent the male and female principles that give rise, in their interplay, to creation.

3   Now concentrate on the heart of the flower with its cluster of circles, like a seed-head. These circles symbolize the divine source of all life, pulsing with energy, as if all the world's plant life has been squeezed to the size of a handful of buttons.

4   Let all the energies of the mandala float deeper and deeper into your consciousness, until your mind achieves a perfect and peaceful resonance.

RECOMMENDED COLOUR PALETTE

CENTRAL CLUSTER OF CIRCLES: **Green** for spring, youth, renewal, freshness, fertility, hope

CENTRAL PETALS: **Yellow** for purity, truth, optimism, fulfilment

BANDED TRIANGLES: Follow your intuition in colouring these. Options might include:

Purple for emotions, self-expression; **Red** for passion, sacrifice, dynamism, strength;

Brown for earth, the physical world, groundedness; **Orange** for beauty, creativity, spirituality

TEAR SPLASHES and BLANK SPACES: **Blue** for tranquillity, eternity, perfection

"EVERYTHING IN THE UNIVERSE IS WITHIN YOU.
ASK FOR EVERYTHING FROM YOURSELF."

JALAL AD-DIN RUMI

(1207—1273)

HEXAGRAM

THE HEXAGRAM IS A PAIR OF INTERLOCKING TRIANGLES, REPRESENTING UNITY IN DUALITY. IN JUDAISM, THE SYMBOL IS KNOWN AS THE STAR OF DAVID AND IS ASSOCIATED WITH SOLOMON. HEXAGRAMS ALSO APPEAR IN HINDU MANDALAS AND CAN BE A POWERFUL FORCE FOR HEALING.

1   Identify the large upward-pointing triangle, which is masculine and symbolizes fire, and the large downward-pointing one, which is feminine and denotes water.

2   Observe the upper part of the upward triangle, with the base of the downward triangle crossing through it: this is the symbol for air. Then look at the lower part of the downward triangle, again with a horizontal bar across it: this is the symbol for earth. The mandala, then, contains all four elements.

3   Take the mandala as a whole into your mind. As you do so, you are absorbing all the elements, all creation. The fifth element, spirit, denoted by the outer circle, is the medium through which your inner life unfolds.

RECOMMENDED COLOUR PALETTE

INTERSECTING TRIANGLES: **Orange** for beauty, creativity, spirituality
CENTRAL UPWARD TRIANGLE (interior): **Blue** for tranquillity, eternity, spirit, perfection
CENTRAL CIRCLE: **Green** for spring, youth, renewal, freshness, fertility, hope
CHEVRONED AREA AROUND HEXAGRAM: **Blue** for tranquillity, eternity, spirit, perfection;
with thin **Yellow** bands for purity, truth, optimism, fulfilment

"THOSE WHO WORSHIP ME WITH DEVOTION,
THEY ARE IN ME AND I AM IN THEM."

THE BHAGAVAD GITA

(C.500 BC)

WORLD TREE

WITH ITS ROOTS AROUND THE EARTH AND ITS BRANCHES
IN THE HEAVENS, THE WORLD TREE SYMBOLIZES OUR ABILITY
TO TRANSCEND OUR HUMBLE ORIGINS IN THE DENSE REALM
OF MATTER AND ASCEND TO HEAVENLY BLISS.

1 Contemplate the World Tree, so vast that its canopy stretches over day and night. The tree's fruits are the good things given to us by the divine – the harvest of virtues, including love, compassion, peace and self-awareness. In your knowledge of this tree and of its fruits, you are immensely privileged. You are aware that, as long as you keep this knowledge in your heart, you will be fulfilling your true destiny.

2 Sense the vital essence of the World Tree, which is both material and spiritual, rising through the trunk and branches as you bring them deep into your mind, and flowing through the channels of your spirit.

3 Understand that if a branch breaks off, the tree still stands. In the same way, your spiritual essence is eternal, whatever accidents befall your body.

RECOMMENDED COLOUR PALETTE

SKY, and OCEANS in globe: **Blue** for tranquillity, eternity, spirit, perfection
LEAVES, and LAND in globe: **Green** for fertility, earth, nature, renewal
STARS and SUN: **Red** for dynamism, strength, desire; **Orange** for beauty, creativity, spirituality;
Yellow for purity, truth, optimism, fulfilment
CLOUDS and MOON: **White** for totality, purity, majesty

"WHEN THE WIND OF PURE THOUGHT RUSTLES AMONG ITS LEAVES,
THE WORLD TREE WHISPERS THE NAME OF THE DIVINE."

MODERN MEDITATION FROM GERMANY

DOVE OF PEACE

THE DOVE IS THE MOST SPIRITUAL OF BIRD SYMBOLS. IN ADDITION TO ITS UNIVERSAL IMPORTANCE AS AN EXPRESSION OF PEACE AND RECONCILIATION, IT CONJURES UP THE PURIFIED SOUL – OR, IN CHRISTIAN TERMS, THE HOLY SPIRIT.

1 Within the outermost circle of the mandala, which indicates perfection, contemplate the continuous, flowing pattern as an image of earthly energies. When you colour in the inner circles, they form a rainbow pattern, a beautiful manifestation of the life-giving spirit of the sun.

2 Now focus on the dove with its olive branch, a symbol of salvation. The dove has materialized out of pure spirit – like your own most profound qualities of love and peace. Hold the bird in your gaze as if you are seeing it through a telescope. The deep, dark background behind it is eternity.

3 Take this dove into your mind, and relax in the knowledge that it is completely at home there. You have recognized its sign, and you welcome the bird and its message of peace.

RECOMMENDED COLOUR PALETTE

FLOWING PATTERN: **Yellow** (*standing in for gold*) for solar power, creativity, spirituality;
against a background of **Purple** for grace, abundance, beauty
DOVE: **White** for purity, innocence, holiness
OLIVE BRANCH: **Green** for triumph of life over death
CONCENTRIC CIRCLES: The colours of the rainbow, **Red**, **Orange**, **Yellow**, **Green**, **Blue**, **Purple** (standing in for indigo and violet), to suggest the never-ending cycle of life and our covenant with divinity

"PEACE BRINGS LOVE AS LOVE BRINGS PEACE.
THE PERFECT FORM IS THE CIRCLE."

MODERN MEDITATION FROM SYDNEY, AUSTRALIA

SNOWFLAKE

THE SNOWFLAKE IS FLEETINGLY BEAUTIFUL – WE SCARCELY HAVE
TIME TO ADMIRE IT BEFORE IT MELTS. SUCH IS THE WAY OF
THE WORLD – OUR LIVES AND LOVES CHANGE ENDLESSLY,
BUT AT OUR CENTRE IS THE UNCHANGING SPIRIT
THAT NEVER DIMINISHES.

1 Look at the snowflake in this mandala, one of an infinite number of snowflakes, yet complete and perfect within itself. Observe its exact symmetry, and be aware, as you appreciate the design, that no other snowflake in the entire cosmos is identical to this one. Let this thought sink into your mind. Spend a few minutes relishing this everyday miracle.

2 Consider the snowflake's intrinsic strength, which comes from its unique beauty. The snowflake is ephemeral, yet flawless.

3 Imagine that the snowflake is on the point of melting. You are observing it in the moment of its being, from the viewpoint of your own fleeting lifetime.

RECOMMENDED COLOUR PALETTE

SNOWFLAKE and CONCENTRIC CIRCLES: **White** for peace, happiness, purity, innocence
BACKGROUND: **Blue** for tranquillity, eternity, spirit, perfection;
with touches of **Green** shading for fertility, earth, nature, renewal
Colour the "commas" within the small central circle according to your own intuition

"WEAK OVERCOMES STRONG,
SOFT OVERCOMES HARD."

TAO TE CHING

(4TH OR 3RD CENTURY BC)

ROSE OF PURE LOVE

THIS MANDALA IS THE ROSE CROSS, A SYMBOL THAT GAVE ITS NAME TO THE MYSTIC ORDER OF THE ROSICRUCIANS. THE CROSS SIGNIFIES THE FOUR CARDINAL DIRECTIONS, WHILE THE ROSE SUGGESTS PURE LOVE AS WELL AS SACRIFICE. THE SUPPORT THAT THE ROSE AND THE CROSS GIVE TO ONE ANOTHER ENHANCES THE SENSE OF COMPLETENESS.

1   First, consider the cross, which anchors the spirit in the physical world. So powerful a symbol is the cross that we can readily imagine its central point behind the rose. It gives support to the rose, whose flowering transcends it. Cross and rose are in perfect balance with each other – an exemplary union.

2   Look at all the petals of the rose, beautifying the world. Think of them as the unfolding of love within your own heart. Although transient, the flower has its time of perfect fulfilment. Its destiny is realized, between the past and the future.

3   Take the entire mandala into your inner self, where the rose will manifest selfless love, compassion and spiritual awareness, founded within the incarnation of the cross.

RECOMMENDED COLOUR PALETTE

LEAVES: **Green** for fertility, earth, nature, renewal
ROSE: **Red** for love, compassion, spirit, sacrifice, strength
CROSS: **Brown** for earth, the physical world, groundedness
OUTER BACKGROUND: **Blue** for tranquillity, eternity, perfection

"THE HEART'S MESSAGE CANNOT
BE DELIVERED IN WORDS."

MU-MON GENSEN

(1322—1390)

ETERNAL FEMININE

THIS MANDALA ENCLOSES FEMININE SPIRITUALITY WITHIN
THE PROTECTIVE WALLS OF STRENGTH AND COMMON SENSE.
AT ITS CENTRE IS THE YONI, THE FEMALE CREATIVE SYMBOL,
HELD LOVINGLY WITHIN THE LOTUS OF ENLIGHTENMENT.

1   First, look at the square around the lotus, with its double-buttressed walls. It is located between emblems of the spirit – the outer circle and the lotus buds, both of which suggest purity and transcendence. The square is the earthly foundation that grounds us and prevents us from losing touch with the everlasting truth. The eternal feminine is both grounded and spiritual, practical and mystical, compassionate and heavenly.

2   Soften your gaze, and let go of all these thoughts you have had about the mandala's symbolism. Let your mind enter the lotus flower and let the lotus flower enter you. While you are meditating upon this mandala, you are absorbing the energies of the eternal, creative, feminine principle, which brings you into the physical world and, at the same time, gives you the gift of intuitive wisdom.

RECOMMENDED COLOUR PALETTE

LOTUS FLOWER: **Pink** for transcendence, spirituality, femininity
YONI: **Red** for love, compassion, physicality; **Yellow** for purity, truth, fulfilment
LEAVES: **Green** for fertility, earth, nature, renewal
OUTER CIRCLE and SQUARE FRAME: **White** for wisdom, purity, longevity
BACKGROUND: **Purple** for grace, abundance, beauty

"FOR A WOMAN IS THE EVERLASTING FIELD
IN WHICH THE SELF IS BORN."

THE MAHABHARATA

(C.400 BC—C.200 AD)

YIN YANG

THE YIN YANG SYMBOL AT THE CENTRE
OF THIS MANDALA IS AN ANCIENT EASTERN IMAGE.
IT REPRESENTS THE BALANCE BETWEEN OPPOSING
FORCES THAT CONSTITUTES OUR WORLD.

1   Look first at the flowers and other motifs set within the main geometric shapes of this mandala. Appreciate the contrast and interplay of the squares and rectangles (the material world) with the circles (eternity).

2   Now turn your attention to the central yin yang image. See how each of the two elements contains the seed of its opposite. Relate this idea to the opposites balanced within yourself: masculine/feminine, action/stillness, insight/compassion, outward/inward, and so on.

3   Look at the tiny yin yang symbols between the outer square and the surrounding circle, touching both – their positioning on the boundary between created and spiritual worlds is significant. Think of these symbols as atoms that occur in everything, the universal stuff of existence.

4   See the mandala with all its embellishments as both the cosmos and the individual cell – each is a mirror of the other, the part and the whole inseparable within a holistic system.

RECOMMENDED COLOUR PALETTE

YIN YANG SYMBOLS: **Red** for the feminine principle, compassion, inwardness, stillness;
White for the masculine principle, insight, outwardness, action
FLOWERS: **Green** for fertility, earth, nature, renewal; **Orange** for beauty, creativity, spirituality
OUTERMOST CIRCLE: **Blue** for tranquillity, eternity, perfection, immortality
OTHER AREAS: **Yellow** for solar power, creativity, spirituality; **Purple** for grace, abundance, beauty

"CLAY IS FIRED TO MAKE A POT.
THE POT'S USE COMES FROM ITS EMPTINESS."

TAO TE CHING

(4TH—3RD CENTURY BC)

STAINED-GLASS WINDOW

THIS MANDALA EVOKES THE HEALING PEACE OF A CHURCH
OR TEMPLE AND CAPTURES THE SUN'S NURTURING RADIANCE:
THE GIFT THAT BRINGS THE BEAUTY
OF STAINED GLASS TO LIFE.

1 See the main three- and four-leaved shapes as symbolic of nature – the universe of infinite forms. The subject of the window is the harmony of the natural world, shown by leaves, flowers (within circles) and bunches of berries (in the corners of the central square).

2 See the pure design taking form as an actual window, which you are observing from inside a sacred building. Appreciate its artistry and workmanship.

3 Lastly, imagine that the window is lit from behind by bright sunlight. All the colours glow beautifully. The window has become a perfect symbol of nature animated by spirit and, at the same time, of human creativity animated by spiritual wisdom. As you draw the mandala deep into your mind, recognize that it reflects the essence of your true whole self.

RECOMMENDED COLOUR PALETTE

EMPTY SQUARE PANES: **Red** for love, compassion, spirit, sacrifice, strength;
Green for fertility, earth, nature, renewal
BUNCHES OF BERRIES (in the corners of the central square): **Blue** for tranquillity, eternity, perfection
SQUARE and CIRCULAR FRAMES: **Yellow** (standing in for gold) for solar power, creativity, spirituality
LEAVES: **Green** for fertility, earth, nature, renewal

"TRUTH AND MORNING BECOME LIGHT WITH TIME."

ETHIOPIAN PROVERB

THUNDERBIRD

FOR NATIVE AMERICANS THE GREAT SPIRIT MANIFESTED HIMSELF
IN VARIOUS NATURAL FORMS, INCLUDING THUNDERBIRD,
GUARDIAN OF THE SKY, WHO WAS ENGAGED IN ENDLESS
BATTLE WITH THE SERPENTS OF THE UNDERWORLD.

1 Look at the great bird in the centre of this mandala: Thunderbird. See this bird as symbolizing the source of active good in the world, the energy that nourishes our virtues and keeps us alert to all moral dangers.

2 Now contemplate the spiral pattern that surrounds the central Thunderbird – representing the endless flowering of creation, the dynamic principle that animates the cosmos.

3 Take the bird's energies into your mind as a totem of your spiritual self-knowledge. Whatever your beliefs, this powerful image of the natural world – a bird at home in the storm – can help you to affirm your purpose. Absorb its natural and cosmic power. Your potential is enlarged. You can now exert powerful transforming energies to heal yourself.

RECOMMENDED COLOUR PALETTE

SPIRAL PATTERN: Narrow bands **Brown** for earth, the physical world, groundedness;
Broad bands **Yellow** (standing in for gold) for solar power, creativity, spirituality
CIRCLE AROUND BIRD: **Red** for love, compassion, physicality; with accents in blue, white and brown
THUNDERBIRD: **Black** for success, power, mystery; **White** for wisdom, purity, longevity;
Yellow (standing in for gold) for solar power, creativity, spirituality

"LISTEN TO THE VOICE OF NATURE,
FOR IT HOLDS TREASURES FOR US ALL."

HURON SAYING

WATERFALL

THIS MANDALA SHOWS LIFE AS A POOL IN THE ENDLESS FLOW OF TIME. THERE ARE DANGERS (THE CROCODILES) BUT IF WE ARE PURE WE WILL COME TO NO HARM. BY ACCEPTING THAT WE ARE PART OF NATURE, WE GAIN SELF-UNDERSTANDING.

1   Start by looking at the source of the waters, high in the mountains. The rainbow is like a halo, symbolizing the beauty and sacredness of life when sunlight (the divine) shines through water droplets (our bodies) in the atmosphere.

2   Now think of yourself as the swimmer, free and naked in the pool. You immerse yourself fully in nature, in the way things are. You rejoice in your being, in your incarnation within a lifetime.

3   You understand that any physical dangers are an integral part of nature, too, which is why the crocodiles in the mandala appear to flow like streams themselves. Accept that the rainbow blesses the crocodiles as well as the swimmer. Life is a constantly changing balance of forces.

RECOMMENDED COLOUR PALETTE

WATER: **Blue** for tranquillity, natural energy, freedom, endless possibilities

GRASS: **Green** for fertility, earth, nature, renewal

TREE FOLIAGE: **Purple** for grace, abundance, beauty

CROCODILES: **Brown** for earth, the physical world, groundedness

SNOW (on mountain peaks): **White** for wisdom, purity, aspiration

RAINBOW: The colours of the rainbow, **Red, Orange, Yellow, Green, Blue, Purple** (standing in for indigo and violet), for the never-ending cycle of life and our convenant with divinity

"BODIES COME AND GO LIKE CLOTHES."

SRI SANKARA

(C.788—C.820 AD)

OCTOPUS

THE OCTOPUS IS A SYMBOL OF THE UNFOLDING OF CREATION
FROM ITS MYSTIC CENTRE, AS WELL AS AN EXAMPLE OF OTHERNESS.
THIS MANDALA COMBINES THESE MEANINGS TO GIVE US
A SENSE OF WHO WE ARE AND WHAT LIFE IS.

1 Look into the octopus's staring eyes and then at the random spirals of the octopus's eight arms. These tentacles suggest the endless energies of life as it unfolds out of the mystic centre of creation. The mystery of the octopus is the mystery of the cosmos itself.

2 Now think of the octopus as a creature with its own brain and its own individual mental landscape – not a mind as such, but a kind of world-view nonetheless. What might it feel like to be an octopus? We will never know: some of the Earth's enigmas will remain beyond our comprehension.

3 The octopus squirts a cloud of black ink around itself to confuse its enemies. But you are not its enemy. You co-exist with the octopus and wish it no harm. Indeed, you respect its vital essence and the validity of the life it leads. Think of the creature's strange beauty as one of the blessings you have inherited at birth – a privilege that is given to you as a windfall. Your world is richer for your acquaintance with this miracle, however enigmatic it remains.

RECOMMENDED COLOUR PALETTE

OCTOPUS: **Purple** for grace, abundance, beauty; add green spots if you wish
FRONDS OF WEEDS and TWO CONCENTRIC CIRCLES: **Green** for fertility, earth, nature, renewal
SEAHORSES: **Green** for nature and renewal; **Yellow** for purity, truth, fulfilment
WATER: **Blue** for endlessness, mystery, freedom, aspiration

"THE ENLIGHTENED SOUL IS OPEN TO WONDER.
EVERY MARVEL OF NATURE MIRRORS THE MIRACLE OF BEING ALIVE."

MODERN MEDITATION FROM LISBON

FLOATING LOTUS

THE LOTUS REMAINS UNTOUCHED BY EITHER THE WATER OR THE
MUD THAT NOURISHES IT – SUGGESTING OUR UNDEFILED SPIRIT.
THIS HEALING MANDALA HAS AN OVERHEAD VIEWPOINT.
THE SWIRLING SURROUND IS TURBULENT WATER –
WITH A CIRCLE OF CALM WATER AT THE CENTRE,
LIKE A LAKE WITHIN A RIVER OR SEA.

1 Look at the swirling oceanic waters of the created world. They have their own divine beauty, and a restless energy – the energy of creation ceaselessly unfolding.

2 Turn your gaze to the central, circular pool of water, containing the lotus. As if by magic, the pool reflects the starry night above – an image of the awesome vastness of the cosmos.

3 Contemplate the lotus at the heart of the mandala, with its central yin yang (or t'ai chi) symbol. The lotus denotes pure spirit, embracing the complementary opposites of our existence.

4 Lastly, let these various beauties – water, sky, stars, flower and our own contradictory natures – harmonize in your mind and bring you peace and well-being.

RECOMMENDED COLOUR PALETTE

YIN YANG SYMBOL: **Blue** for the feminine principle, compassion, inwardness, stillness;
Red for the masculine principle, insight, outwardness, action
LOTUS FLOWER: **Pink** for love, empathy, spirituality, divinity
CORNER LEAVES and GRASS: **Green** for fertility, earth, nature, renewal
SWIRLING OCEAN or RIVER: **Blue** for change, weather, freedom, emotion

"THOSE WHO KNOW THE TRUTH ARE NOT EQUAL
TO THOSE WHO LOVE THE TRUTH."

CONFUCIUS

(551—479 BC)

SUN LOTUS

THE CENTRE OF THIS MANDALA IS A SOLAR SPIRAL WITHIN A CLEAR BLUE SKY. THIS IS PLACED WITHIN A LOTUS, WHICH DEPICTS BEAUTY GROWING WITH ITS ROOTS IN THE MUD OF A LAKE, JUST AS THE SOUL RISES FROM CONFUSION TO ENLIGHTENMENT.

1 Look at the outside of the mandala, the circle, which suggests eternity. Then contemplate the open lotus flower, a symbol of spiritual perfection within that heavenly frame.

2 Now turn your attention to the heart of the mandala. The spiral here could represent the meditator's journey into the self – as well as the primal flow of energy that makes the world what it is.

3 Feel how you relate to these different elements: the perfection (outer circle) that you can find within yourself if your heart is pure; the flowering of spirituality from the soil of incarnation (lotus); the energy of the sun (spiral), which drives your earthly being.

4 Let these elements fuse together in your mind, as in the totality of the mandala. Find peaceful self-awareness in this thought.

RECOMMENDED COLOUR PALETTE

CENTRAL SPIRAL and OUTER CIRCLE: **Red** for passion, spirit, sacrifice, strength;
Yellow for purity, truth, fulfilment
LOTUS FLOWER: **Pink** for love, empathy, spirituality, divinity; use white and red as well
for a more varied effect
BACKGROUND: **Blue** for tranquillity, eternity, perfection

"WITHOUT SELF-KNOWLEDGE WE ARE SUNDIALS IN THE SHADE."

MODERN MEDITATION FROM ROME

FLUTE PLAYER

THE FLUTE PLAYER IS AN IMAGE USED BY THE 13TH-CENTURY PERSIAN POET RUMI TO SYMBOLIZE OUR LONGING FOR UNION WITH THE SPIRIT. THE FLUTE YEARNS TO JOIN ITS SOURCE – THE REEDBED FROM WHICH IT WAS ORIGINALLY CUT.

1 Look at the flute player playing at sunset. Behind him are the clumps of reeds from which the flute was cut. Imagine that the music, the flute and the player are all one, responding yearningly to the call of the divine.

2 Think of the flute player's music as a soundless expression of his unconscious mind – a flowering of the soul in its purity. The music is like the call of a child for its mother – innocent and impassioned.

3 Now turn your attention to the other forms of life in the mandala – the waterlilies and fishes. Think of these too as yearning for unity: all the cosmos is one, a vast system of interconnections, animated by the life-force. Absorb all these energies into your meditating mind, and let them rest there – the whole within the self, the self within the whole.

RECOMMENDED COLOUR PALETTE

FLUTE PLAYER and FISHES: **Orange** for beauty, creativity, spirituality
SUNSET: **Red** for passion, yearning, aspiration
ISLAND, REEDS and BACKGROUND TO MUSICAL NOTES: **Green** for fertility, life-force, divinity, renewal
LOTUS FLOWERS: **Pink** for love, empathy, humanity
WATER: **Blue** for tranquillity, eternity, perfection

"PURE SOUL, HOW LONG WILL YOU TRAVEL?
YOU ARE THE KING'S FALCON. FLY BACK TOWARD THE EMPEROR'S WHISTLE!"

JALIL AL-DIN RUMI

(1207—1273)

FLOWER OF SELF

THIS IS A MANDALA IN WHICH TO LOSE AND FIND ONESELF.
IT REFLECTS FLOWERING SELF-AWARENESS, THE ETERNAL SELF
IN FULL BLOOM, THE UNCHANGING ESSENCE AT THE CORE
OF ALL OUR REPEATED DAYS, WEEKS, MONTHS AND YEARS.

1   Visually trace the wave-like spiral shoots that surround the central flower. They are lines of energy, each of them a wave of becoming, revealing within itself a flower of being. The bees are in perpetual motion, their wings beating faster than the eye can see.

2   Now turn your attention to the central flower. Take its many-petalled radiance into your mind, where it rests as a still reflection of your many-petalled self, the flowering of the eternal present, the essential truth of existence, the life-force that animates the cosmos.

3   There are two bees on the petals of this central flower, but you do not brush them away: you are happy to let them live their fleeting moments on the wonderful flower of the spirit – like our own lifetimes within the vast cycle of all creation, and, on a smaller scale, the cycle of earthly birth, growth, life, death and renewal.

RECOMMENDED COLOUR PALETTE

MANY-PETALLED FLOWERS: **Yellow** for purity, truth, fulfilment, solar energy, optimism
SPIRAL SHOOTS and LEAVES: **Green** for fertility, earth, nature, renewal
CIRCULAR BANDS (around flower-heads): **Blue** for tranquillity, eternity, perfection

"TRUTH IS INSIDE YOU. TO SEE IT YOU MUST OPEN THE INNER EYE."

THE BUDDHA

(C.563—C.483 BC)

STAR IN THE WELL

LOOKING DEEP INTO OUR SELVES WE SEE OUR GREATEST RICHES –
SUGGESTED BY A STAR REFLECTED IN THE WATER AT THE BOTTOM
OF A WELL. LIKE ANY STAR, IT IS UNTOUCHABLE BUT REAL.
IT GIVES US EVERYTHING AND NOTHING. IT IS THE OBJECT OF
ALL OUR QUESTING.

1 Identify the different stages and planes of the mandala: the outer world of nature, the circular surround of paving, the square base within that, the inner ring of paving, and lastly the hollow drop of the well itself.

2 Contemplate the star that you can see reflected in the water of the well. It shines brightly despite the darkness and the distance. See it as a beacon of hope, an affirmation of the cosmic miracle.

3 As you continue to focus on the star reflected by the water within the well, think of yourself as looking right into the innermost depths of your own spirit. The deeper you penetrate, the brighter you shine. Your star is unique and beautiful, and can never be extinguished.

RECOMMENDED COLOUR PALETTE

STAR: **Yellow** for purity, truth, divinity, mystery
PAVING: **Brown** for earth, the physical world, groundedness;
alternating with **Green** for fertility, life-force, renewal
FOUR FLOWERS: **Pink** for love, empathy, humanity
LEAVES: **Green** for fertility, life-force, renewal

"AS FAR AS WE CAN DISCERN, THE SOLE PURPOSE OF HUMAN EXISTENCE
IS TO KINDLE A LIGHT IN THE DARKNESS OF MERE BEING."

JULIAN OF NORWICH

(1342—C.1416)

DOLPHINS AT PLAY

THE DOLPHIN IS PLAYFUL AND COMMUNICATIVE.
IT TAKES JOY IN EACH MOMENT INSTINCTIVELY,
AND USES THIS AS INSPIRATION FOR WELL-BEING.
DOLPHIN SYMBOLISM IS COMBINED HERE WITH IMAGERY
OF THE OCEAN, FROM WHICH ALL LIFE EVOLVED.

1 Look at the dolphins swimming in the centre of the mandala and the two dolphins performing acrobatics around them. Their ability to break free of their own element, the water, and dance in another, the air, suggests our own potential for liberation once we have embraced the power of the spirit.

2 Contemplate the circle that the two dolphins make in their dance of joy. The circle suggests both spiritual perfection and the endless cycle of life, rising and falling, coming and going, like the dolphins.

3 Turn your attention to the four conches in the corners of the mandala. Each is a miracle of evolution, a token of the genius of life itself, in all its myriads of forms.

4 Think finally of the vastness of the ocean, and the infinite expanse of sky above it. Taking the mandala as a whole into your mind, absorb the harmony of the cosmos. Our lives are gleaming droplets of water within the shining ocean of being.

RECOMMENDED COLOUR PALETTE

WATER and SKY: **Blue** for tranquillity, spirit, freedom, infinity
Use different shades of blue if available: light for the sky, dark for the sea
TURBULENT FOAM and CLOUDS: **White** for purity, truth, innocence, divinity
CONCHES: **Red** for the life-force, passion, blood; with white surrounds

"GRACE IS A GRAVITY THAT HAS LEARNT HOW TO PLAY."

MODERN MEDITATION FROM LOS ANGELES

WATER GARDEN

A GARDEN IS THE UNIVERSAL SYMBOL OF HARMONY
IN NATURE AND OF THE HUMAN SOUL WHICH,
JUST LIKE A GARDEN, MUST BE IN HARMONY WITH ITSELF
IN ORDER TO FIND PEACE.

1 Concentrate first on the element of water. The life-giving powers of the water, which plays endlessly through the fountain, give sustenance to the fish, just as love gives sustenance and strength to the soul.

2 Now turn to the structure within which the water is contained. The paving around the pond is made up of uneven blocks fitted together perfectly – a symbol of the work done by unconditional love and of love's tolerance of imperfections.

3 Lastly, notice that you cannot focus on all four of the trees that flourish outside of the garden at once, but that you can hold them at the edge of awareness, just as love can contain all things. Think of love as the soil, rain and roots of existence.

4 Softening your gaze, take the mandala as a whole into your mind, and let it rest there as an emblem of wholeness, whose energies permeate through your unconscious mind.

RECOMMENDED COLOUR PALETTE

FISH: **Orange** for beauty, creativity, spirituality
WATER: **Blue** for tranquillity, spirit, freedom, infinity
PAVING STONES and DOLPHIN SPOUTS: **Grey** for potential, uncertainty, origins
GRASS, FOLIAGE and PLANTS: **Green** for fertility, life-force, renewal
CIRCLE OF FENCING: **Brown** for the man-made world, restraint, boundaries, groundedness

"YOU ARE AN OCEAN OF KNOWLEDGE HIDDEN IN A DEW DROP."

JALIL AL-DIN RUMI

(1207—1273)

JACOB'S LADDER

IN THE BOOK OF GENESIS, JACOB DREAMS OF ANGELS ASCENDING
AND DESCENDING A LADDER BETWEEN HEAVEN AND EARTH.
EVEN IN OUR PHYSICAL EXISTENCE WE CAN ENJOY AND
BENEFIT FROM INTIMATIONS OF THE DIVINE –
PROVIDED THAT WE ARE OPEN TO LOVE.

1 Start by gazing at the earthly city at the base of the mandala. Its inhabitants are caught up in their various preoccupations. Few of the city-dwellers even notice the ladder to Heaven: it exists on a different plane from the mundane.

2 Now look at Heaven, at the top of the mandala. Its gates are within you, ready for you to enter – just as the mandala itself will be within you when you absorb the whole image into your mind.

3 Look at the angels moving back and forth between Heaven and Earth. Their love for the divine, and the love shown by the divine to them, keeps them airborne. Think of them as messengers showing you the way to fulfilment and peace.

4 Lastly, review the journey ahead, up the ladder and into the spiritual world. The angels will help you. Love provides the energy.

RECOMMENDED COLOUR PALETTE

LADDER and GATES OF HEAVEN: **Yellow** (standing in for gold) for aspiration, creativity, spirituality
NIGHT SKY: **Purple** for divinity, beauty, majesty; alternatively, use black or dark blue
STARS and ANGELS' WINGS: **Yellow** for optimism, fulfilment, mystery
CLOUDS: **White** for purity, truth, innocence
ANGELS' ROBES: **Red** for joy, spirit, service, strength
EARTHLY CITY: **Grey** for potential, emptiness, imperfection

"BE NOT FORGETFUL TO ENTERTAIN STRANGERS,
FOR THEREBY SOME HAVE ENTERTAINED ANGELS UNAWARES."

HEBREWS 13:2

ISLANDS

NONE OF US IS AN ISLAND – WE ARE ALL JOINED TO EACH OTHER BY BRIDGES OF THE SPIRIT, AND ARE STRENGTHENED IN THE PROCESS. HERE IS A MANDALA THAT TRANSLATES THIS UNIVERSAL METAPHOR AS A JOURNEY FROM THE ISOLATION OF THE UNENLIGHTENED SELF TOWARD THE COMMUNITY OF FAITH.

1   The starting point is the Earthly city, at the base of the mandala. Think of its millions of individuals, all with their unique lives and circumstances, dreams and worries. All are strangers to you.

2   Now think of an archipelago of desert islands. Each has people stranded on it, refugees from the overcrowded city. They stand at different ends of their islands, unable to connect with each other.

3   In your mind, set out on a voyage to each island in turn to bring its inhabitants together in neighbourly love. Do this through the power of your own love for all humankind.

4   Finally, take the whole mandala into your heart. See the islanders smiling at each other rather than looking out to sea.

RECOMMENDED COLOUR PALETTE

ISLANDS: **Yellow** for solar energy, truth, divinity, mystery
PALM TREES: **Green** for fertility, life-force, renewal
WATER: **Blue** for tranquillity, spirit, freedom, infinity
CITY BUILDINGS: **Grey** for potential, emptiness, imperfection; with yellow windows
SAILS OF JUNKS: **Orange** for beauty, creativity, spirituality

"THE ONLY WAY TO HAVE A FRIEND IS TO BE ONE."

RALPH WALDO EMERSON

(1803—1882)

SAILING THE STORM

STORMY SEAS HAVE TESTED THE FORTITUDE OF COUNTLESS SAILORS. THIS MANDALA SHOWS A SHIP IN PERIL. USE IT TO FIND YOUR OWN RESERVES OF COURAGE, AND AS A SPIRITUAL COMPASS WITH WHICH TO PLOT A SAFE COURSE.

1   You are looking down on a sailing ship from a bird's-eye view. You are safe, dry and calm, but the ship is in trouble – buffeted by gigantic waves, sails threatened by lightning, torrential rain lashing down on the crew.

2   Next scan the mandala as a whole, and notice its harmony. Appreciate that a world where ships can be lost to violent storms is still a beautiful world, and that even in extreme danger you have the resources of spirit to give you strength.

3   Look at the four compasses in the mandala – your tools to steer by. Perhaps these are love, faith, acceptance and compassion.

4   Now look again at the mandala as a whole. See it as reflecting life's totality, with all its challenges and contradictions.

RECOMMENDED COLOUR PALETTE

SHIP: **Brown** for endurance, simplicity, resolution, courage
SWIRLING OCEAN: **Blue** for life-force, change, the unconscious; **Green** for nature, fertility, growth
NIGHT SKY: **Black** for infinity, mystery; or dark blue if available
STARS: **Yellow** for cosmic energy, truth, divinity
LIGHTNING, DOVES and CLOUDS: **White** for purity, transformation, completeness

"ONLY THAT WHICH CANNOT BE LOST IN A SHIPWRECK IS TRULY YOURS."

AL-GHAZALI

(1058—1111)

SAMURAI SWORD

THE SWORD IS A SYMBOL OF AUTHORITY AND DECISIVENESS.
THIS MANDALA SHOWS A SWORD-GUARD SURROUNDED BY FOUR
SWORDS AND THEIR SCABBARDS. MEDITATE ON IT WHEN
PREPARING FOR A LIFE CHANGE OR A BOLD DECISION TO ENSURE
YOU HAVE COMPLETE CONVICTION IN YOUR ACTIONS.

1 Look at the central circle and, within that, the decorative cross of the sword-guard – an image of creation within spiritual perfection.

2 Now turn your gaze to the swords and scabbards. Unsheathed, the swords indicate the decisions you need to make and your willingness to act on those decisions in a timely fashion. Contemplate the edges of the swords, and imagine testing their sharpness very carefully with your fingertips.

3 Lastly, make your decision to act in the way that you believe is right. Focus your will on moving through the centre of the mandala – the egg-shaped hold in the centre of the sword-guard. The flowing embellishments around the sword-guard suggest right action, in accordance with natural law.

RECOMMENDED COLOUR PALETTE

SCABBARDS: **Red** for passion, yearning, aspiration
SWORDS: **White** for purity, innocence, action
SWORD-GUARD: **Yellow** for solar energy, truth, divinity, mystery
BACKGROUND TO SWORDS AND SCABBARDS: **Blue** for tranquillity, spirit, freedom, infinity
PATTERNED CORNERS: **Orange** for beauty, creativity, spirituality

"CONFUSIONS AND DANGERS ARE NOTHING BUT THE MIND."

DOGEN

(1200—1253)

CONFRONTING THE MINOTAUR

THE MINOTAUR, A MYTHICAL BULL-LIKE CREATURE THAT LIVED IN A
LABYRINTH ON THE ISLAND OF CRETE, STANDS FOR ALL OUR
INNER DEMONS – ATTACHMENTS, FEARS, FAILINGS IN LOVE.
THROUGH MEDITATION WE CAN TAME THE MONSTER.

1   Think of the Minotaur as a source of negative energy that you need to defeat. As you enter the maze, you unroll a thread from a spool: this is your connection with the world of safety, your knowledge that the Minotaur can never really harm you.

2   Trace your way through the confusion of many turnings – you are moving deeper and deeper into the depths of your being. As you do so, your illusions fall away, one by one, and your awareness becomes heightened.

3   When at last you reach the centre, you find that the Minotaur is already harmless. What took courage initially was facing the truth about yourself. Now that you confront the truth, you do so in a spirit of total acceptance. You are at peace.

4   Now, softening your gaze, take the mandala into your mind – maze, thread, bull and all. You contemplate all this in a spirit of enlightened detachment. All anxieties and harms are banished to the realm of illusion.

RECOMMENDED COLOUR PALETTE

MINOTAUR and BLANK SPACES, including the corridors of the labyrinth:
Brown for endurance, simplicity, resolution, courage
WALLS OF LABYRINTH: **Yellow** for progress, challenge, mystery
THREAD: **Red** for good fortune, destiny, strength
(colour a narrow band along the winding thread shown as a black line)

"IT IS NOT BECAUSE THINGS ARE DIFFICULT THAT WE DO NOT DARE,
IT IS BECAUSE WE DO NOT DARE THAT THEY ARE DIFFICULT."

SENECA

(C.4 BC—65 AD)

CAUSE AND EFFECT

IT IS SAID THAT WHEN A BUTTERFLY FLAPS ITS WINGS IN JAPAN,
IT CAUSES A HURRICANE IN LOUISIANA. TO SEE THAT ALL THE
WORLD'S EVENTS ARE CONNECTED IS TO UNDERSTAND THAT WE
SHOULD ALL TAKE RESPONSIBILITY FOR OUR ACTIONS.

1   Look at the three interconnected gear wheels. They are an obvious form of cause and effect.

2   Now look at the butterfly, whose wings flap metaphorically to create a storm on the other side of the world. This is an example of a cause producing its effects invisibly. Such unseen connections occur throughout existence.

3   Focus on the mandala as a whole: its asymmetrical form around an inner wheel conceals the harmony of the cosmos. In the same way, any imbalances in our own lives conceal the unified whole of the spirit.

4   Finally, softening your gaze, contemplate the hub of the central wheel. Take deep into your consciousness the awareness that all life revolves around a still central point. Let this thought lie lightly within you.

RECOMMENDED COLOUR PALETTE

CENTRAL WHEEL: **Yellow** for solar energy, truth, divinity, mystery
SECONDARY WHEELS: **Brown** and **Blue**, the colours of earth and sea, creation and infinite space
BUTTERFLY: **Red**, **Yellow** and **Blue** for life's variety and wonder
SWIRLING BACKGROUND (*within outer circle*): **Green** for nature, fertility, growth
OCEAN: **Blue** and **White** for realistic effect

"THROUGH WHAT IS NEAR,
ONE UNDERSTANDS WHAT IS FAR AWAY."

HSUN-TZU

(C.300—C.238 BC)

PAGODA OF SPIRIT

THE PAGODA ADDS A SPIRITUAL DIMENSION TO THE JAPANESE GARDEN, DEPICTING OUR ASCENT TO HEAVENLY BLISS THROUGH STAGES OF ENLIGHTENMENT. THIS MANDALA ALSO SYMBOLIZES THE BALANCE BETWEEN NATURE AND ARTIFICE.

1 View the pagoda as a succession of separate temples, one built on top of another. This is the triumph of art over formlessness, yet its purpose is not to aggrandize humanity but to assert the vitality of the spirit – creativity employed in the service of the divine.

2 Notice that the pagoda has open sides, beneath the deep overhang of the eaves. The building is a meeting-point of emptiness and solidity.

3 Contemplate the uppermost level, with its pointed roof. This symbolizes spirit – the crowning glory of the created world. Whatever stage you are at on your journey, you can see your destination clearly. All the ladders on which you will climb are already present and there for the finding.

4 Softening your gaze, take the whole mandala into your mind as an image of harmonious, multi-layered reality.

RECOMMENDED COLOUR PALETTE

TEMPLE ROOFS: **Green** for nature, fertility, growth, tranquillity
FLOWERS: **Pink** for love, empathy, humanity
SKY and LAKE: **Blue** for infinity, potential, freedom
CLOUDS: **White** for purity, truth
CIRCULAR SURROUND: Choose colours according to your intution

"LOGIC WILL GET YOU FROM A TO B.
IMAGINATION WILL TAKE YOU EVERYWHERE."

ALBERT EINSTEIN

(1879—1955)

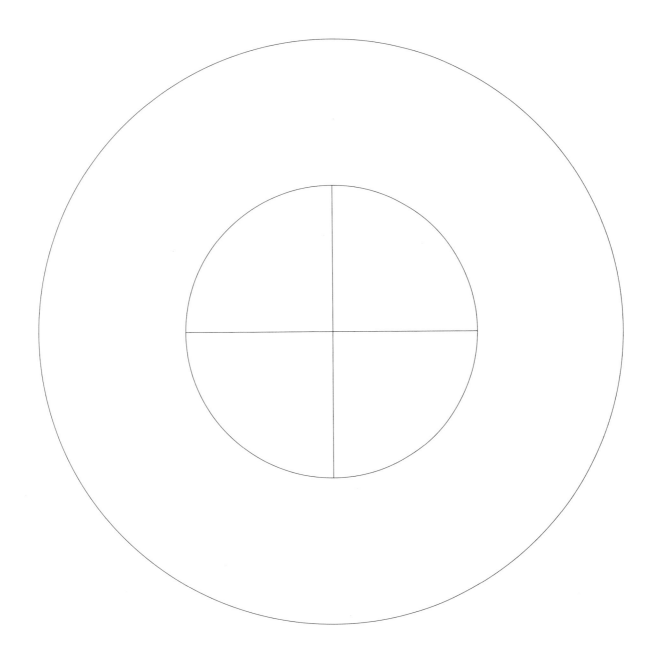

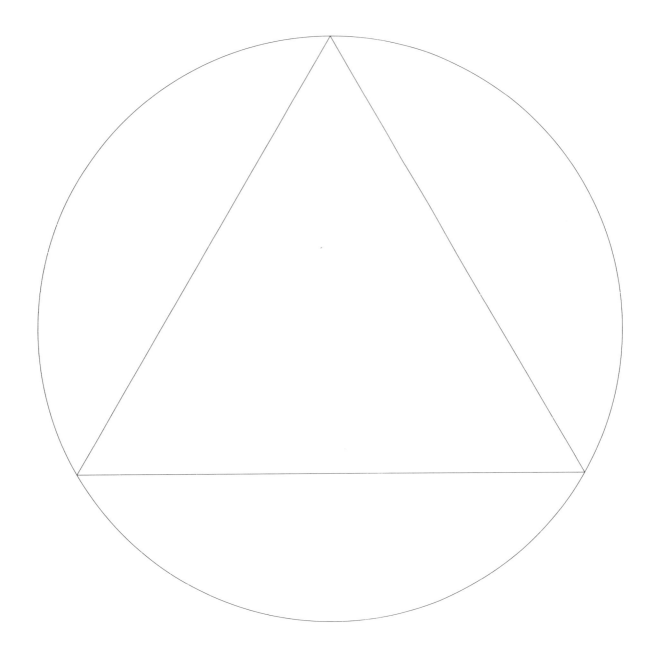

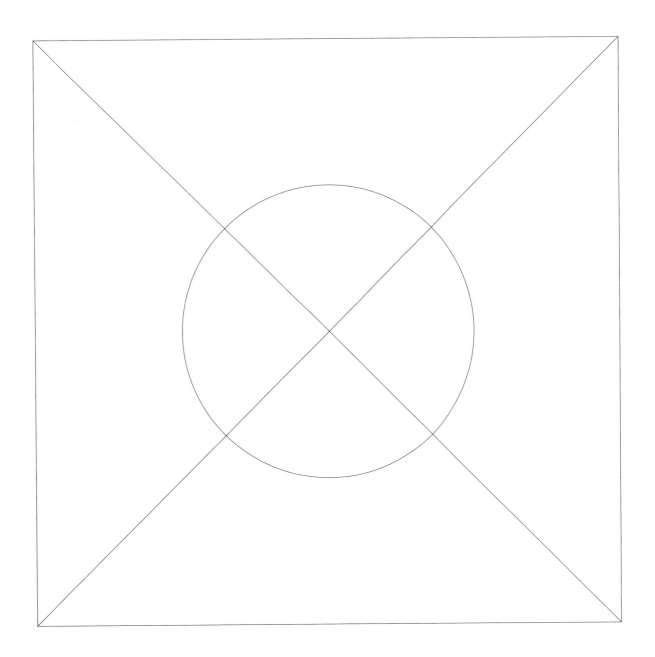

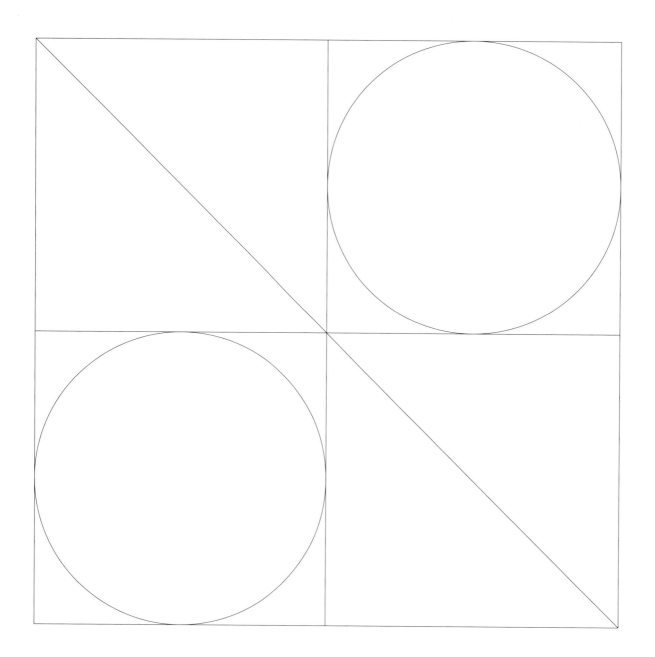

SYMBOLS OF HEALING

Images are more ancient and universal than alphabets, words or writing, for they tap into our collective unconscious. Throughout history and all across the world they have been used to express feelings, provoke reactions, tell stories and embody philosophies – as well as to heal and increase a sense of connection with nature and with our spiritual source.

Although the meanings of symbols vary to some extent from culture to culture, our shared experience as human beings – principally an experience of nature and of the human life-cycle – has generated a universal language of symbolism. Because motifs such as a tree, a flower, water, fire, sun and moon, and dolphins at play in the ocean speak to people intuitively, regardless of race or creed, they offer great potential for exploration in healing. These symbols form the basis of many of the mandalas in this book.

Also universal is the symbolic geometry of the mandala: the circle that is endless, the triangle that suggests a flame, the square that signifies the created world. Other, more culturally rooted symbols – the Egyptian Eye of Horus, the Sanskrit Om symbol, the I Ching hexagrams of China – have an intrinsic beauty and long-lived significance that endow them with a universal potency.

Geometry is a key element in mandala symbolism. The mind is drawn to geometric shapes, which, as objects of meditation, help to establish a positive framework for our thoughts. Free of explicit representational content, geometry has a purity that enables it to work well as a mental resting place. Yet at the same time, it can be rich in implications. It offers ways of visualizing, for example, the interaction of spirit and flesh (the cross) or the concept of eternity (the circle).

Nature is a source of inspiration and value. We are inspired by the vastness and intricacy of a cosmos that lies forever beyond our control. We find beauty and profundity when we lose ourselves in the contemplation of life-forms that are beyond total understanding. In mandalas, the deeply symbolic associations of plants, and sometimes animals, speak to us at a level that transcends cultural differences. To some extent, a tree or a flower has general significance related to nature's cycles, while animals tend to represent the Other, a self that is emphatically not our own. But when we consider individual families or species of plants or animals, a more specific symbolism comes into play – for example, the association of pine trees, in Japanese tradition, with longevity, or the cat, in Western tradition, with instinctive pliability and subtlety.

Each time you meditate on the mandalas in this book, keep your mind open to the full range of possible interpretations. One image can carry a number of associations – the rose, for example, can stand for love, beauty and compassion. Your response to a motif at any moment will reflect not only your world-view, your cultural background and your knowledge, but also your changing moods. This aspect of variability adds depth to mandala meditation and enlarges its healing potential.

DIRECTORY OF HEALING MANDALA SYMBOLS

Mandalas tend to be formed around a central point, known as the *bindu* – Sanskrit for "point" or "dot". A meditation will often culminate in the practitioner focusing deeply on the centre and losing his or her sense of identity in total absorption. Around the central point there is scope for various kinds of healing symbolism. The elements, for example, have universal positive significance: water is life-giving and liberating (it frees us from gravity); air is the essence of breathing; fire purges us of harmful habits; and earth keeps us grounded. Animal symbolism can make available to us the attributes of various creatures with powers that go beyond our own – such as birds, with their gift of flight; lions, tigers and bears, which possess immense strength; and the butterfly with its ability for radical transformation. A healing mandala may also borrow from centuries of accumulated spiritual symbolism within various traditions of both East and West: the lotus, the rose, the star, the cross, the ladder to heaven and the yin yang symbol (see p.71) all fall into this category, their meanings multi-layered and profound.

Bee
A symbol of fertility and sexuality, promising fulfilment within the cycles of life.

Crocodile
Like fire, the crocodile is not merely destructive; it can be helpfully purging.

Seahorse
A symbol of wonder and mystery, reflecting the life-force within the cosmos.

Pagoda
A place of refuge, healing and harmony, with aspirations toward spiritual bliss.

Bridge
A transition toward wellness, wholeness and fulfilment, achieved by enlightened action.

Minotaur
The demon within the self – our base nature, which courage and love enable us to tame.

Star in Well
The treasure of spirit in the dark depths of our being, like a star reflected in the water of a well.

Dove
A divine messenger of redemption, and a reason to have faith and hope.

Butterfly
A universal symbol of change, and the unfolding of spiritual perfection.

Yin Yang
The complementary balance of opposites – here shown within the lotus of the spirit.

Thunderbird
In Native American belief, a vision of infinite power and divinity.

Samurai Sword
A symbol of decisiveness – including the will to overcome adversity.

Fish
A creature with many meanings, including prophecy, intuition and the feminine.

Island
A place of potential solitude, surrounded by the ocean of healing and peace.

Jacob's Ladder
The dissolution of boundaries between Earth and Heaven – a mystic vision of eternal reward.

HEALING MANDALAS
LISA TENZIN-DOLMA

First published in the UK and USA in 2013 by
Watkins Publishing Limited
Sixth Floor
75 Wells Street
London W1T 3QH

A member of Osprey Group

Osprey Publishing Inc.
43-01 21st Street
Suite 220B, Long Island City
New York 11101

Editor: Rebecca Sheppard
Managing Designer: Sailesh Patel
Commissioned Artwork: mandala colour artworks
by Sally Taylor/ArtistPartners Ltd; line illustrations
for mandala templates by Studio 73

IBSN: 978-1-78028-600-6

10 9 8 7 6 5 4 3 2 1

Typeset in Novecento wide, Filosofia and Gill Sans
Colour reproduction by PDQ, UK
Printed in China

Publisher's note: This book does not recommend
meditation with mandalas for the specific treatment
of any disability, only for the enhancement of general
well-being. Meditation is beneficial for most people
and generally harmless, but those unsure of its suitability
for them should consult a medical practitioner before
attempting any of the meditations in this book. Neither
the publishers nor the author can accept responsibility
for any injuries or damage incurred as a result of
following the meditations in this book, or using any of
the meditation techniques that are mentioned herein.